This is dedicated to:

ALL THE AMAZING
ALMOST
KINDERGARTENERS.

D1706494

It is almost time
for me to go
to Kindergarten!
Am I Ready?

Yes I am!

I am ready.
I can
write my name!

_____
- - - - - - - - - - - - - - - - -
_____
- - - - - - - - - - - - - - - - -
_____
- - - - - - - - - - - - - - - - -
_____
- - - - - - - - - - - - - - - - -
_____

I am ready.
I can
say my ABC's!

A B C D E F G
H I J K L M N
O P Q R S T U
V W X Y Z

I am ready.
I can
say some
letter sounds!

I am ready.
I can
count to 10!

1 2 3
0 5 8 4
9 7 10 6

I am ready.
I can
color a picture!

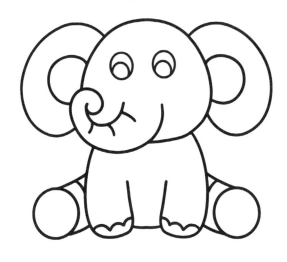

I am ready.
I can
hold a pencil!

I am ready.
I can
name my shapes!

I am ready.
I can
name my colors!

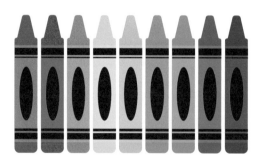

I am ready.
I can
play safe
at recess!

I am ready.
I can
go to the bathroom
all by myself!

I am ready.
I can
sit at the carpet!

I am ready.
I can
cut safely with scissors!

I am ready.
I can
eat my lunch
in the cafeteria!

I am ready.
I can
take turns!

I am ready.
I can
name what
I am feeling!

I feel green because I am going to school!

I am ready.
I can
raise my hand!

I am ready.
I can
leave my class
and go to
Music, PE and Library!

I am ready.
I can
share!

Sharing is Caring.

I am ready.
I can
put my jacket on!

I am ready.
I can
use glue!

A LITTLE DAB WILL DO!

I am ready.
I can
stand in
a straight line!

I have waited
all summer.
Now, it is time
to be a Kindergartener!

I AM READY!

This book belongs to:

_____

_ _ _ _ _ _ _ _ _ _ _ _ _ _ _ _ _ _ _

_____

_ _ _ _ _ _ _ _ _ _ _ _ _ _ _ _ _ _ _

_____

_ _ _ _ _ _ _ _ _ _ _ _ _ _ _ _ _ _ _

_____

_ _ _ _ _ _ _ _ _ _ _ _ _ _ _ _ _ _ _

_____

Kindergarten is a magical year
full of many firsts.
I wish you and your family the very best.

With Love,
Mrs. Woods

About the Author:

Kira Woods has been a Kindergarten teacher for 13 years.
She was a social worker before she was a teacher.
She has three grown daughters.
She lives in Washington with her husband
and their two dogs.

Made in United States
Troutdale, OR
05/18/2024

19949845R00017